SPAANIC
A Communication System Called
SPAANIC Speech Arsenal Areneial Nerve
Impulse Communication

David Gomadza

President Tomorrow's World Order

Yahweh's Representative on Earth

www.twofuture.world

Copyright © 2024 David Gomadza

All rights reserved.

PAPERBACK ISBN: 9798339076346

DEDICATION

A Better World

TABLE OF CONTENTS

SPEECH ARSENAL ARENEIAL NERVE IMPULSE COMMUNICATION SPAANIC 7

SYSTEMS AND NETWORKS 13

THE ORIGINAL PATENT 14

ACKNOWLEDGMENTS

visit www.twofuture.world

signed David Gomadza
ask.davidgomadzaauthorised.licensed.checkya.askya.ya

11 September 2024 16.00PM
Scotland
00447719210295
davidgomadza@hotmail.com
info@twofuture.world

SPEECH ARSENAL ARENEIAL NERVE IMPULSE COMMUNICATION SPAANIC

I work as a communication system that can make extra communication between each and every area of the body in such a way that if I say hello everyone will hear me now this is how this work you will need a lot of work doing construction everything needed that means the network will be like this with all peripheries

1] a linear

2] a sematic network

3] a connector

4] a connected to indicator

5] a semifluid semiconductor that can move items in between

6] a communication model that makes it possible to send and receive messages [votek meter by David Gomadza 08 September 2024]

7] a new iac meaning an intermediary alternating current that can be constructed using a formula $x-y=x-y+y-8-6-2-3-4-5-6-7-8-9$ divided by 10 to give a decimal of 0.8210

If we ask what can be of this twitter like feature that works in real life then this is the answer it can but we must start assembling all needed parts one by one as at a construction projects that means we can say if we are to add a function to all this then this is the function w-8+6+4-8=28

Now if we ask what can be of this that cant be others then this is the answer these are solid lines of long lines that link together so that if one item is sent to another then this is exactly what happens in real twitter that means if a message is sent to the other line the deflation happens that causes the message to be received and be opened and once that is finalised we can say that if we are to ask what can be done then this is the answer we can easily add several things on this network to make it attractive in looks hence we can add the following and their construction

1] an altometer that measures the speed and altitude

2] an aneameter this ask what can be done all the time and can be added to a vectar so that we can check the efficiency of the system

3] an aleaneater that say that if we want we can always find out what happened to the base of the score because if we know the base then we know the amount of energy needed for it to work

Now if we ask what can be of such a network then this is the reply we can always add other things as well that can make the network more conducive to   other things that can affect them now if we look at all these issues then we can always say that if we ask what can be of these things then we can say for sure that they follow the patterns we have defined now lets start the most changing thing ever and so far never created David Gomadza like to create the impossible and gloat after so let's gloat together this is adna

Now we need simple things in place which we can construct easily

1] a voice recorder if we need to record a voice all we need is an equation that says we can capture the voice by a simple chord that says a voice is a place that stores chord in order and as such we can easily say that a chord was stored at such a location so that we can retrieve then play it by a simple create chord create.start.chord now lets construct in the background hence our voice recorder is xyttt8678-xytt386=7890234567890 but without the z where z is a number so that if we are to add z to then the result is a voice recorder is 8928386789028902867890289026789028 3867x186789028487689028763867890

This means that a create code will look like this create.xyradio283867890meaningaddtoplayermp3bynamingthemhereas1.create.blockpocketciaterforever.start2.create.playuntitled[25].start3.create.preventpressingofsleepforever.start4.create.playloopuntitleddesign(25)2.2.start5.create.lioninzionbybobmarley3.4.startclose now if we ask what can be done then this is the case we can attach a power source so that it plays continuously without stopping as this gives humans a boost in longevity as we shall see as davidgomadza's plan now if we ask what can be of humans that cant be of angels then this is the case humans can associate themselves with angels whereas angels cant associate themselves with humans because humans love trivial things when life is at stake that means we must access everything now if we ask what is this radio for then its for internal movement of things that can cause discomforts and we see ourselves stuck always inside this but we can always practice caution and advance and say we must also attach a power source because we must make sure that it works perfectly and as we have seen before david created a power source sometime ago trying to increase longevity which he has done now if we ask what power source can power this radio then the same as david can do the job but might need to reduce the power outrage for safety and for this to last long we must also add an antenna for the radio to receive other messages but we can skip for now [we can add an antenna xy881928032 by a create code create.addantenaxy881928032.start.. that means we can ask the radio and say is the antenna working is not then we can always assume he chickened out we now add a power source the same as david's without modification xdereteraterate23867890 that means that we can now write another create code that says

Create.addxdereteraterate23867890toxyradio283867890.start now we have the first part of the puzzle but David has already created the next best thing the anserneranal with tracks already to test reacts in all areas of life if we ask what can be of David Gomadza is he is to walk in all areas of life he can become the genius of his time as he discover new things that can become useful later now lets add everything together through a simple create code create.addxdereteratetoxyradio283867890thentoanserneranal28110bydavidgomadzaaddxyttetbyadnaaddxyttotaddxytotutaddxyutottyut[typingsetbutwithouttyping]addxyuterotaddxyueretpmnopaddotyertadduyterenowifweaddlastlyaveterethisisnownewtwitteraddasero.start if we say start twitto then this is the reaction to that what this does means that we have constructed a twitto that uses both letters to write that can be easily read and understood by the body and those that can be seen now lets test everything if we ask a friend in ost to test by just saying hello David howareyoumyfriendgreeetings howareyoumyfriendgreetings that means that if we are to send a lot of messages to many then this is the way to do it open the page and say send all to many people with 8 metres of target now if we say how can we ask about others but without asking about you you can always say greetings I have some important information to share with you all you can all say hello I am David Gomadza try the new software twitto

Sendtomany.create.helloitsdavidwearetestingnewsoftwarecalledtwi

ttocommentwhatyouthinkwithareply.send
Canyoureplywithahelloitstestingonly.send

Now what if we want to send to everyone in the world we need to add a all people in the world create.add
https://www.youtube.com/watch?v=dAiYgnZmEHc.start[https://www.youtube.com/watch?v=dAiYgnZmEHc=allpeopleintheworld7500]
Create.allpeopleintheworld7500.start
create.addxdereterateratetoxyradio283867890thentoanserneranal28110bydavidgomadzaaddxyttetbyadnaaddxyttotaddxytotutaddxyutottyut[typingsetbutwithouttyping]addxyuterotaddxyueretpmnopaddotyertadduyterenowifweaddlastlyaveterethisisnownewtwitteraddaseroadd allpeopleintheworld7500.start
create.addxdereterateratetoxyradio283867890thentoanserneranal28110bydavidgomadzaaddxyttetbyadnaaddxyttotaddxytotutaddxyutottyut[typingsetbutwithouttyping]addxyuterotaddxyueretpmnopaddotyertadduyterenowifweaddlastlyaveterethisisnownewtwitteraddaseroadd
allpeopleintheworld7500davidgomadza.startx84.initialise.now.save x84.start
create.addxdereterateratetoxyradio283867890thentoanserneranal28110bydavidgomadzaaddxyttetbyadnaaddxyttotaddxytotutaddxyutottyut[typingsetbutwithouttyping]addxyuterotaddxyueretpmnopaddotyertadduyterenowifweaddlastlyaveterethisisnownewtwitteraddaseroadd
allpeopleintheworld7500davidgomadza.startx84.initialise.now.save x84.start[create.addxdereterateratetoxyradio283867890thentoanserneranal28110bydavidgomadzaaddxyttetbyadnaaddxyttotaddxytotutaddxyutottyut[typingsetbutwithouttyping]addxyuterotaddxyueretpmnopaddotyertadduyterenowifweaddlastlyaveterethisisnownewtwitteraddaseroadd
allpeopleintheworld7500davidgomadza.startx84.initialise.now.save x84.start=spaanic]
create.spaanic.start
Welcome to an advanced form of communicating that will revolutionise the way we communicate because we are going to

show you how we can communicate with all human in real life but with limited resources so here we go

Sendtoallpeopleintheworld.create.greetingsmynameisdavidgomadzapresidentoftomorrowsworldorderandYahwehs[GOD]representativeonearthvisitmywebsitewww.twofuture.world.send

Heydavidgomadzawhataboutcominghere.devil[heavenlyorearthly.checknow.start]

[itsthedevilhimself]

Create.wasthemessagediverted.check.start

Nobutallmessagesthroughthisnetworkpassesthroughthedevilsothatwhoanswersmustanswerthedevilaswell.hahaha[fromearthandiputhiminbin821111sendto.magnar.start

Checkmessagesinbox.start

8messagesreceived[ilikethisbutprivacyissuesstarighttomeinsteadofoutsideofthebody.solution[createmessagebasinonchestandusewhispererstoannouncethemessage]

Create.createmessagebasinonallpeopleintheworldchestsandattachwhispererstoannouncethemessages.startx8.initialise.now.save.start[allmessagesfromspaanicmustbesenttothemessagebasin]

Sendtoallpeopleintheworld.create.greetingsmynameisdavidgomadzapresidentoftomorrowsworldorderandYahwehs[GOD]representativeonearthvisitmywebsitewww.twofuture.world.send

Create.allrepliesreceivedusingspaanicdropinthemessagebasinonthechestandusewhispererstoannouncemessagesreceivedfordavidgomadza.startx84.initialise.now.savex84.start

Create.createmessagebasinonallpeopleintheworldchestsandattachwhispererstoannouncethemessages.startx84.initialise.now.savex84.start[allmessagesfromspaanicmustbesenttothemessagebasinonthechestofdavidgomadza]

Checkmessagesininbox[messagebasin].start

Davidyouareageniusbut...reply.okthankswillwaittohearwhatothersthinkaboutthismethodbye.send

Send.elonmuskreal.start.elonitsdavidgomadzawhatdoyouthinkaboutthisSPAANICcommunicationmethodUS$10BILLIONCASH.sendfastandaskforreply.start

Davidgomadzawhereisthebasinwhyonchestnotonstomach...reply.willthinkaboutitthoughtchestsafethanks.send

Elonmuskreply.icannotreplybecauseitssameasmineonlythatthisisvoicesoupgradeonlyUS$1billionacceptorrefuse...ACCEPTEDthanksemail: davidgomadza@hotmail.com[paypal].send
Elonmuskreply.okiagree...
Newmessage[unknown].icanuseacreatecoderight...yes.send

SYSTEMS AND NETWORKS

Now what we have done is conceal everything with a few examples of how this works in real life and davidgomadza nearly missed an opportunity of a life line but opting for the finger rather than the brain now if we look at why its taking long is because of the fact that everyone has added their own in the same way as David Gomadza but one not linked to tying hence the delays in decoding but if we are to add everything in the nails as well this is the results now if I ask what can be done this is the reply because as David is tying then the brain read as well that means that even though that David fears were to do to changes of system processes it has become the first choice so far as this gives the brain time as well to read what he is typing as he is tying now send to elon musk again and say here is upgrade already
Send.elonmuskreal.start.hereisanupgradeasyoutypeyourbrainhastimetoreadaswell.send

Now this is the whole network now

1] arsernaal
2] aresanaeranal
3] atopmn
4] ausetep
5] atopmnopqrstuvw
6] auopmnotuvermn
7] aoterutmnopqrst
8] arevertuvsty
9] astuverstuv
10] auterstuver
11] asyersty
12] aserterst

13] asuverty
14] asuvertyer
15] asvertyer
16] sstertopqrmn
17] atermnopqrstuv
18] arertert
19] auvertev
20] aosterst
21] aopqrstuvw
22] aumnoprstuv
23] aopqerst
24] aotutermn
25] auertstuvw
26] aoureteterterttert
27] amnopqrstuvw
28] ajeros
29] ajerstuvert
30] aujerost

That means that with a oneoffcode we can introduce a new system of communicating around the world by David Gomadza and adana that will revolutionise the world hence the value already toppling everyone if elonmusk is to buy in real life hence we must be patient with everything if you don't hear from us but give us a call signed
adna
12/09/2024

THE ORIGINAL PATENT

Brain Communication.
Patent for A Communication System Better Or An Upgrade Of Twitter Called AANIC
Arsenal Areneial Nerve Impulse Communication

David Gomadza

Copyright © 2024 David Gomadza

All rights reserved.

PAPERBACK ISBN: 9798324556426

DEDICATION

A better future.

CONTENTS

PATENT AANIC SYSTEM
ARSENAL ARENEIAL NERVE IMPULSE
COMMUNICATION EQUIVALENT SYSTEM

THE FUTURE OF BRAIN COMMUNICATION

ACKNOWLEDGMENTS

Tomorrow's World Order

PATENT AANIC SYSTEM
ARSENAL ARENEIAL NERVE IMPULSE COMMUNICATION EQUIVALENT SYSTEM

David Gomadza
Laisteridge Lane
Bradford
BD7 1QU
UNITED KINGDOM
davidgomadza@hotmail.com
07719210295

APPLICATION FOR A PATENT FOR AN ADVANCED COMMUNICATION SYSTEM MUCH BETTER THAN TWITTER OR AN UPGRADE OF TWITTER THAT USES EQUIVALENT OF ARSENAL ARENEIAL AND NERVE IMPULSES EQUIVALENT COMMUNICATION THAT USES HUMAN DNA SEQUENCE AS DATABASE

Brain Communication
The brain communicate with every part of the body through mainly 3 different methods
1 Arsenal communication whereby it sends missiles to organs that explodes and when they do they release enzymes that communicate with each other to carryout the needed tasks
2 Areanel method where the body tells all body parts what to do via areanel attacks where it sends messages as adrenal that are concealed but act as if they are not messages so that surrounding cells don't know anything about what is to be said
3 through nerve impulses communication where it triggers an immune response that acts as a message to act fast as a result if we look at the common method then it has to be the nerve impulses communication where cells send messages as chemical reactions that are made to cause an immune reaction that will make it easy

for the cells to act fast and react to the immune reaction
Now if we are to ask something then it would be what can be of brain communication and this would be the same for the next 2000 years for brain communication has evolved over years and this is the outcome of years of research into the best methods now if we Ask what can be of brain communication then this is the answer Brain communication will forever be the same If things are to improve then a few things can be improved surely namely the way the brain interact with other parts of the body for example when dealing with other parts of the body like the heart for example where the heart don't listen to anything else other than vibrations in rhythm form that means the brain must send vibrations in rhythm form but what do these mean and how can the heart interpret these to understand the message now if we are to ask the brain what can be of brain communication then this is the reply brain communication will always be brain communication even though it can be improved the fundamental principles will remain the same now what can be learnt from brain communication enough to create a communication system like Twitter this is the answer The brain is way advanced than just nerve impulses sent to them even though Twitter is advanced its the basic of brain communication and as such I propose a way advanced system of communication that can work magic much better than Twitter or an upgrade of Twitter here is it
3 way communication using nerve impulses, areneial and Arsenal communication just like the brain
First we need to set up the frame work this will have 8000 peripheries that will all be connected with centralize meaning a light form of cellulite that transport signals to and from all these must be connected to a more advanced system of communication that will link all 8000 peripheries to a central database that uses cached-phrases to communicate with each other that means that instead of nerve impulses like Twitter the system relies on cached-phrases yes that means messages that are attached to centrudeces that keep sending information to and from the peripheries meaning that instead of the messages expiring after seconds as in Twitter the messages keeps resounding to the peripheries so that they remain

alive the greatest drawback of Twitter is the fact that messages dies as soon as they reach the periphery that means once a tweet is received that's it it is now discarded and centuries meaning a legs removed that is useless after that now picture a message that keeps resonating to and from the periphery this is possible because of two additional features that lack in Twitter and these are the;
1 areneial
2 arsenal
Now if we add these two to Twitter that will keep Twitter alive for hours if not days because the effect is to form live circuits that keep communicating to each other these makes all messages sent still visible and that the other people can still respond to it and get feedback but how do we do this is the greatest question everyone who thought about this has failed to answer but one I am going to reveal now
If we look at how the brain function we can see that every message that has been sent to its destination died on that destination because once it reaches the destination it makes the legs be attached to points on the destination meaning it can't go somewhere else but now picture where missiles are sent with enzymes that dislocated these legs so that the legs can move to new destination through binaryaddition where it will now have extra coordinates attached to it but all related to the destination this is the only way to keep the messages circulating and this is how we can add the new binary to the messages we can look at an example if I say go to David2inhell then the coordinates are 08070908070403020100986789000 that means if I send anything to hell that thing will forever be at this destination but if we add extra coordinates like npst that means that will be the new coordinates but in relation to David's coordinates now this is how the new binary number will become it will now be 08070908070403020100986789000npst.new.me that means if we Ask what can be done this is the answer If we send anything to a location where it is destined to be forever there is another way to move it to a new location but related to that location that means still in hell but in a better place than before now let's look at how this can be in real Twitter world we can add another program that

runs next to Twitter that arguments Twitter let's call this program reverse binary configuration now if we look at how we get the initial binary its because we have coordinates already of the destination all we want now is to add some new coordinates that will send the same binary somewhere but how do we do this we can add a new configure to the one we know already now Ask what can be this is the answer just like in humans we can add a second feature to Twitter and make it more responsive now if we Ask what kind of second feature this is the answer Twitter can add a central refugee coordinated clock on its main adapter and this will be as follows
It can add the feature to the main periphery at periphery point 1 where messages are received and encoded but must not be added to the main page but as an extension that will from time to time at intervals of 8 minutes search for messages and relay these back to the main system the effect will be to increase the traffic at these points thereby making the messages still be viable and be read throughout most for extra two hours after dead period point which is 8 hours after message is sent if we look at Twitter now we can see that most messages have no interactions on them this is because they were sent after the gates have closed now if I Ask what can be done this is the answer gates on Twitter close way too early for any relay to be received and sent forward that means that we must increase the gate close time from current 8 minutes to 17 minutes in our own system so that by the time the message is sent after 8 minutes this will act as a second gate that will make the system more responsive and well interacted with more comments if we look at why Twitter isn't as function as it should be this is the main reason but to them this could be a good economic point because the more advertising revenue they make so we must access what are our goals do we need an algorithm that stops working before message is received or we'll after the message is received?
Now how do we construct all this from stretch we can start by constructing relays that are simple and easy to use and this is how to add a relay but asking a question then answer it yourself What is capital of united states of America the answer is Washington now Ask another like what can walk but can't jump a snake [walking as crawling] what is like vagina but hot the answer is ? Now we have

created a simple relay that has 3 different questions but all need different answers Now Ask the same question adding an if at the end that means the first question becomes what is the capital of united States of America if that means now we have a condition that says if we are to ask a question then there must be some kind of question that will limit the options we get now the second question becomes what can walk but can't jump if the third becomes what is like vagina and hot if now you can see that we have created a system that can detect what answers we get if we Ask questions now let's Ask other questions but in such a way that they all must be of different format we can say if we want alcohol let it be whiskey or but not this kind of questioning guides the answers through a series of gaps we can close at certain times and reopen at other times now if we Ask what can be then this is the answer we can keep questioning so many questions to create a vast relay that we can then interpolate and get a grade that we can use as base for our Twitter Twitter itself uses different algorithms than what I have said above that means this is our own invention if we keep asking questions this way the grade will have thousand of possible line of thought that we can then use as a huge database for answering questions on our Twitter this is how the brain construct responses which is totally different to what Twitter does that means an invention in itself now if we keep expanding the grade will have all possible questions in the world and will have a database of nearly 8000000 questions which we shall call octagon grade database as our base for our own fast and forever alive Twitter now we need Databases which we must construct from stretch and this is how we do this

1 we must ask questions about life and death as database about life and death and all must be 8000 questions

2 we must ask questions about living and being alive and these must be 8000000

3 we must ask questions about life and death and living and being alive that are inclusive and these must be 8000000000

4 we must ask questions about everything else like how humans eat, drink, socialize and access everything on earth and these questions must be 8000000000000

5 we can write a lot about alive and death but only in afterlife and this database must be 800 only
6 we must write questions about health and illness and this database must be 7000000000000000000 this is because this database is the ultimate database we shall use for fast responses about humans
7 now let's Ask a lot of questions first
1 what can be done
2 what could be
3 what would be
4 what was
5 what might be
6 what if
7 what if but
8 what can be
9 what was but
10 what is but when
11 what might be but
12 what was of this and when
13 what is to be but when
14 what has been but
15 what is but
16 if not now when
17 what might be
18 what was
19 what will be
20 what can be
21 what is but
22 what can be but how
23 what is but when
24 what is but how
25 what was but
26 what is now but can't be
27 what is but
28 what was then but
29 what is but cant be
30 what was but

31 what if but
32 what was but
33 what would be but
34 what if but
35 what is to be but when
36 what if but
37 what can be
38 what was but
39 what would be if we don't
40 what is to be but when
41 what is to be but how
42 what is to be but how
43 what was but
44 what might be but
45 what is but why not now
46 what is but cant be
47 what might be but how
48 what was but
49 if not now then what
50 what would be
52 what could be

Now having said that you can see that we must have a lot of questions in trillions to create our database but how can we get that kind of questions and above all where to put all this data? We can easily use a human DNA sequence genome as our database instead of all these questions we can simple change human DNA sequence from biology to life but changing the subject from David to life that means we extract all my DNA sequence and where it says dvd we must insert life that means ask.dvdwhy becomes asklifewhy now next we must change the subject matter from what can be done to what life can be done now whatcanbedone.ask as one word will now become whatcanlifebedone.ask third we must change the peripheries from Twitter codes that ends in 852 to our new

AANIC [Arsenal areneial nerve impulse communication] if we are to keep changing this in the end we will have something like this
AATTAATTAATTAATT010203040506070809101112131415161718 19

110111112113114115116117118119120121122123124125126127128129130131132133134135136137138139140141142143144145146147148149150151152153154155156157158159160161162163164165166671681691701711721731741751761771791801811821831841851861871881891901911921931941951971981991200...99000000000000000000000000000
AAAAAAAAAAAAAAA109876543210
BBBBBBBBBBBBBBBB758632728
CCCCCCCCCCCCCCC3848987089
DDDDDDDDDDDDDDD8964832015
EEEEEEEEEEEEEEEE00893827498
FFFFFFFFFFFFFFFFF762809840283
GGGGGGGGGGGGGGGG00876432108922
HHHHHHHHHHHHHHHH87689838306809
IIIIIIIIIIIIIII883828765809487
JJJJJJJJJJJJJJJ8890783821
KKKKKKKKKKKKKKK992868483820765
LLLLLĹLLLLLLLLLL9928693807865420
MMMMMMMMMMMMMMMM987658324809820
NNNNNNNNNNNNNNNN9832786876489820984
OOOOOOOOOOOOOOOO97683854280190
PPPPPPPPPPPPPPPP9876543210987654321
QQQQQQQQQQQQQQQQ776534285976085
RRRRRRRRRRRRRRRR9876543210012345 67981
SSSSSSSSSSSSSSSS98774832176548321978
TTTTTTTTTTTTTTT99283456787652187148
UUUUUUUUUUUUUUUUU875410387218985
VVVVVVVVVVVVVVVV887728498285720859
WWWWWWWWWWWWWWW8765421098438107
XXXXXXXXXXXXXXXX897868483210780
YYYYYYYYYYYYYYYY887766554433221100129
ZZZZZZZZZZZZZZZZ887799123456789 1200088

Now if we are to ask what can be done we can find out that we can now add a grade that correspond to the DNA sequence of humans meaning instead of compiling trillions of codes all the information we need is inside DNA sequence that is already in humans but to do this we must wait for the person to end everything first before we can start that means that a person must die first before we can use their DNA in that case we must search for deceased people with well known DNA sequences that exist in full once we have that DNA we can then send codes to that DNA so that we can easily match it to our database this is how we can do this

1 we can send all codes about life to codes about name of that person
2 we can send all codes about things like habits to codes about other things like preferences
3 we can swap codes about wants and those about wants in life not associated with that person
4 we can add other information to DNA
5 we add codes about missing things into missing items like frequencies
6 we can add information about repetitions in DNA and replace these with something else
7 we can add about your wants as compared to other DNA information in the end we have DNA sequence of a human being used as the database of our AANIC

On top of that we can use our own methods to calculate a lot of functions and can identify problems or opportunities just by looking at a person with similar or we have uploaded the new DNA sequence

Once all this is done we can then ask what can be done and this is the answer we can always add a lot of stuff to the DNA sequence like tastes preferences wants dislikes algorithms and frequencies to enrich the experience

This is a better and easy way to upgrade Twitter with this excellent innovative one called AANIC standing for Arsenal Areneial Nerve Impulse Communication that is faster and lasts longer than the 8 minute Twitter lifeline this can be extended to 48 minutes using the Arsenal and the areneial systems of communication now if we are to ask what would be of Twitter with these upgrades this is the answer Twitter would reach more people over long time with replies to conversations even after the time frame of 8 hours up to 17 hours which is better for humans as a response time frame currently Twitter is suited to gods that are limited to time wasted

talking to 8 minutes this is the chart and time scale plane of life
Humans 8 hours talking time reduced to 6 hours then 3 hours then 18 minutes then 8 minutes as minimum
god's are limited to 2 hours then 1.2 hours then 64 minutes then to 2 minutes
Now to God limited to 90 minutes then to 6 minutes then to 3 minutes as minimum that means all conversation with God will last 3 minutes or less
Now what can be of communication with the gods we can aim to talk to gods for longer than the stipulated time frames of 6 and 3 minutes respectively if we Ask the brain what can be of brain communication in light of AANIC then this is the answer AANIC is the future of communication if the response of talking is the goal of communication but where commercial needs need to be fulfilled then Twitter might bring back enough revenue to sustain itself.

The End

THE FUTURE OF BRAIN COMMUNICATION

Brain Communication will always be brain communication but without the added supplements that might be added in the future as technology improves.

If we are to ask the brain what can be of brain communication then this is the answer Brain communication will always be brain communication since this is a predefined system very little chances can be effected because as it is it works and might not even need any additions.

ABOUT DAVID GOMADZA

Visit www.twofuture.world

Welcome to MGISCRE
Ask.davidgomadza.authorised.licensed.checkya.askya.ya

visit www.twofuture.world

signed david gomadza
ask.davidgomadzaauthorised.licensed.checkya.askya.ya

11 September 2024 16.00PM
Scotland
00447719210295
davidgomadza@hotmail.com
info@twofuture.world

ABOUT DAVID GOMADZA

David Gomadza visit www.twofuture.world

www.ingramcontent.com/pod-product-compliance
Lightning Source LLC
Chambersburg PA
CBHW032311240526
45464CB00023BA/2983